THE URGE TO TRAVEL LON DISTANCES

THE URGE TO TRAVEL LONG DISTANCES

Robert Bly

Eastern Washington University Press
Spokane, Washington

Eastern Washington University Press gratefully
acknowledges that several poems were originally
included in *Saturday Nights in Marietta*,
a private edition published in 1999
by the Minnesota Center for the Book Arts.

Designed by A.E. Grey

Library of Congress Cataloging-in-Publication Data

Bly, Robert.
The urge to travel long distances : poems / by Robert Bly.
p. cm.
ISBN 1-59766-010-8 (letterpress edition)—ISBN 1-59766-004-3 (pbk.)
I. Title.
PS3552.L9U74 2005
811'.54—dc22
2005004436

In memory of James Wright

TABLE OF CONTENTS

3 0050 05716 0904

FOREWORD

Robert Bly's poems here, as they evoke both privacy and
closeness to other beings and nature, contain his
characteristic mystery—a fruitful kind that leads us on toward
new territory in the poems' experience and our own. The
poems pulled me strongly, and I was glad to be able to arrange
their publication with Eastern Washington University Press for
the Seventh Annual Get Lit! Northwest Literary Festival.

It is a pleasure to recognize those who created the Festival, and to
thank Robert Bly for making available these poems written,
in the openness of spirit that runs through his singularly influential
career, "to give some honor to the old Chinese poets." Special
appreciation is due to Ivar Nelson, head of Eastern Washington
Press and organizer of the Festival, along with the Press's
Senior Editor, Christopher Howell, and distinguished designer
Amy Grey, in bringing together this commemorative volume.

Peter Nelson
Editor
Altadena, February 2005

INTRODUCTION

I lived as a child on a farm in western Minnesota, which I left in
1944 when I enlisted in the Navy. After the Navy and college
and a few years in New York, I returned in 1955 to a farm a half mile
from my childhood home as a young married man. I wasn't
farming, but my wife and I were simply living in a farmhouse on
some land my father had saved for me. I was amazed at the
permission the land gave to be untroubled, to spend long hours doing
nothing, to pay attention to the wind and the land only a few
years removed from prairie. By then I had found the Chinese poets,
and my models were the poems of Tao Yuan Ming. I modeled
my poems on his relaxed poem songs, but the deep culture
he came from was probably missing in my poems. I gathered a group
of these countryside poems for the collection called *Silence in the
Snowy Fields*, which I finished in 1961. A number of poems still
half-finished remained in manuscript form, and I added a couple of
poems a year over the next few years. During those years, the
Vietnam War was intensifying, and a number of poems about that
suffering were included in *The Light Around the Body*, published
in 1968. So what we have here are a few of the poems written and
left in manuscript during that quiet time before the Vietnam
War claimed our attention. Even in these poems I occasionally see a
hint of the larger suffering:

Late at night the farm resembles a houseboat
Moored on the river, about to slip away.

I still admire the beauty of the Chinese models, which often give
more attention to the beings of nature than to the disasters
of human life.

Robert Bly
Minneapolis, November 2004

THE URGE TO TRAVEL LONG DISTANCES

SINGING LATE AT NIGHT AT CHUCK AND PHIL'S FARM

While the green corn smolders in hazy summer,
We stay up singing by tables under trees.
What should we be doing?
There must be something!
And the one I love is lost among thieves!
Half the night around the table at Chuck's farm,
We sing "Red Wing," and "If I Had the Wings of an Angel."

SPRING NIGHT

Tonight, after riding, and translating a few poems
    from the Danish,
I sawed off wild shoots from the box elder trees.
In the spring night we are not content to be home.
We have urges to travel long distances in the misty dusk.

THE MOON

A solemn moon, nearly full, stands in the east,
Where we imagine Palestine to be.
A few birds fly by. It is the sort of night
When children do not go home for supper.

The fence posts walk slowly around the field.
One post has a stone weighing it down.
Some mower, tired of having it in his sickle,
Lifted it there, balanced it, and left it.

Isn't it possible the moon is a stone
Balanced poorly on a fencepost?
Perhaps some day a man walking alone
Will find the moon by surprise in the grass.

SATURDAY NIGHTS IN MARIETTA

1.

Wonderful Saturday nights with girls
Wandering around! New
Farm machinery standing
Quietly in the cool grass.

2.

Men admire the old timbers
Of the bridge for steadfastness.
But some young women find
These timbers far too mild.

3.

The girl by the theater seems
Cool—like crisp leaves that have just been
Raked together. And all the other
Girls nearby going up in heavy smoke.

SUMMER

1.
The moon hangs in mist over the sleeping corn.
I sit in the ecstasy of the late night
And listen to the crickets cutting up the night
Into small bits of darkness that are food for man.

2.
I remember everything that has happened like a long tail.
I see valleys cooled by pines in the Black Hills,
Cold and powerful moons, grass swaying at night,
Smoke with the odor of straw piles and burnt stubble.

3.
You will find your own image in the grain of wood,
In the dark translucence of trees in summer,
In the rooster's shadow, in the simple chanting
Of a jointed insect, and the kindly shine of screens.

GNATS

This cloud of gnats resembles
Ghost substance—
It changes
Shape, lifts or sinks.

They are too excited—
They can't be feeding.
So few days to live
And they spend it this way!

THE HILLS NEAR DARKY, WISCONSIN

We are nearing these stumpy hills
Of Wisconsin, with oaks on top.
Brown leaves surround each oak trunk,
Like something seen in deep sleep.
I grow dizzy and do not know why:
Round hills, greenish on the slopes,
Becoming brown at the top,
Rising from the wintry cornfields.

A COLD RAIN IN MAY

1.
Outside the rain falls steadily.
It is the earth going to sleep.
The earth is tired and the grass tired;
Now they move toward a cold sleep.

2.
It's like the sleep of water
In a well on some abandoned farm,
Water that will wait and wait
In the clay, and never see the light.

FISHING BULLHEADS WITH LOUIS SIMPSON

1.

I am writing these words with a pencil stub
I found today pressed under dirt near the car tire.
After midnight, I sit down on the stoop.
No badgers are around, the tips of the grass do not move.

2.

The full moon passes under clouds in the south,
Like a flashlight passed under a boat.
The horse stands moodily by the lilacs.
No branches move; the low bushes are still.

3.

Bullheads we caught at Marsh Lake Dam
Thrashed around all day in a ten gallon pail.
At supper, you and I saw they were still alive;
We put them back into a creek nearby.

4.

What does this say? That persistence finally wins out?
That cruelty diminishes after dark? It is summer.
Late at night the farm resembles a houseboat
Moored on a river, about to slip away!

THE VISIT OF TWO BIRDS

1.

The hawk sailed over the trees with the light
    through his wings!
What a joy I received when I looked up and saw
The hawk floating past with the sun through his wings!

2.

The air is clear. It is early summer.
The sun is passing through our bodies also.
That which made it clotted is gone.

3.

At noon I drove north thirty miles.
I found a place by the lake to be,
And sat there alone all afternoon.

4.

After I'd been alone four hours,
A heron, with the cry of those
Who awkwardly suffer, and are ignored,
Settled near me on the shore.

LOOKING AT SOME RUTS A MILE FROM HOME

1.
Rain fell all night, and now
Water stands in the ruts of the farm road.
Turning I see the mud gleaming in two paths,
Going back where I came from.

2.
Where did I come from?
Two farm people, one weighted down with shortcoming,
The other light, eager and feathery,
Married to each other.

3.
I stand a long time
Looking at the two ruts running between mud
Eastward. A car last night, passing, pushed white
Pebbles up the rutsides.

4.
I've made a mess of things.
Whom can I blame?
Not either of these two,
Riding in their heavy car.

WHAT OLAF BULL SAID

Believe in happiness, Seiglinde, try!
                              —Olaf Bull

Happiness is the wind rising
In a field of young plants.

It is a new-fallen apple
Found in the dark earth

Far from the orchard
In plowing time.

OCTOBER MAPLES

How much energy in the weeping willow
Blown by October winds!
The pines hold in their thoughts
And the little maples long for old men.

FLOATING ON THE NIGHT LAKE

The moon rolls on through the eastern sky,
High over the lake and the snowy earth.
How much the moon sees from its place in the sky!
It is just east of us, near the house of great light.

For James Wright

TALK AND LOW CLOUDS
For James Wright, 1961

1.
Clouds and talk. All afternoon while it rained
We talked: of Lorca, the broken father, children lucky
To get out of the house alive. Dark clouds hover above,
Massive, still rich with cold water.

2.
You gone, I see wisps of mist hurrying eastward
Eighty feet or so off the ground, passing
High over my head, wisps misty and frail,
Stark against the solid cloudbank higher up.

3.
These bits of mist seem bodies that expected to get
By without being seen, who celebrate now
Some triumph over the human race, and will return
Tonight to a single pine box in a closed room.

4.
I feel some fear in these layered clouds
That are traveling in the same direction as your bus.
A chill wind starts up; the west says it saw nothing.
Even the tassels of the corn look crude and earthbound.

NOVEMBER

1.

I galloped through the clover at dusk,
Over cold plants touched by frost.
In the west, the sun was setting ocean-
Ward toward its bed of black mussels.

2.

The tired farmer sinks deeper in sleep
And sees the tangled metal, the belt-buckle
Of his regiment, now bloodied on the boy
Caught in the teeth of the thresher.

3.

Geese call all night from the dark.
Half awake in the night, the sleeper hears
Gravestones flying through the stars.
The grass stiffens when the rabbit is gone.

4.

The cold pickerel snouts slide downward
Through layer after chilly layer.
In the orchard, frost-bitten apples fall
To the black heaven underneath the frozen grass.

FARM SCENES

1.

Snow falls in the feeding lot
All afternoon. Everything is white
Except for the dark lumps of hay
The horse has pushed away with his nose.

2.

We talk for hours. Long after midnight
I carry water to the chickens.
The flashlight sways over the snow
Like a single thought alone in the night.

3.

One rooster and five molty hens
Shift uneasily in their stall. The barn
Is shadowy—one or two
Strands of hay hang from the horse's jaw.

A GIFT

I love once more what I have always loved—
Leather, thick and stiff, the odor of clover,
A wooden tongue between two horses,
Frozen mud in the farm yards.

FALL NIGHT

Fall night: Assyrian cities
Of blackbirds asleep in the trees.
Rabbits stretch up, eating the late leaves.
Water goes farther down into the earth.
Clouds cover half the Milky Way.

FEEDING THE HORSES

The blizzard starts. By dusk China's eyelashes
Are white. As I open the barn door, she follows
Me in. Her snow-blanket cracks and flakes off.

Elizabeth, Coltus, then Katherine, all
Step quickly in as if someone were behind them,
Bend their necks down, and eat from the bales.

Wind blows snow sideways across the yard.
Snowbanks change position from one hour
To the next; night appears unexpectedly here and there.

The trees are asleep. Only the barn remains awake.
Snow has sifted onto the chicken feed.
The chickens shift nervously; their roost seems too long.

As I put my hand on the house door, I look back and see
The water tank upturned for winter in the feeding lot.
It's all right. Our bodies will surely last the night.